CW01431704

Original title:
Yewen Clamps Beneath the Griffin Snip

Author: Johan Kirsipuu
ISBN HARDBACK: 978-1-80562-331-1
ISBN PAPERBACK: 978-1-80563-852-0

The Grasp of Dreams in Chain and Sorrow

In twilight whispers, dreams entwined,
A chain of sorrow, hearts confined.
The stars, they weep, in silence deep,
While hope flickers, a flame to keep.

Yet through the night, a spark ignites,
A path unfolds, amidst the blights.
With courage drawn from shadows past,
We seize the dawn, our fears outcast.

Every tear a tale retold,
In chains of dreams, our spirits bold.
We weave our fate with threads of light,
And break the dark, embracing bright.

When Shadows Cloak the Flight of Fate

When shadows cloak the skies so gray,
And whispers drown the light of day,
The winds of change begin to stir,
A quiet heart, a hidden spur.

The jagged paths, where shadows tread,
Lead forth the courage, soft yet spread.
We rise like echoes from the void,
Defying fate, our fears destroyed.

Beneath the cloak, the truth awaits,
As light breaks through the heavy gates.
With every step, the veil rescinds,
And in the dark, our journey begins.

The Resolution of the Feather's Embrace

In feathered dreams, we find our peace,
A soft embrace that bids release.
Through every trial, our spirits soar,
In gentle whispers, we explore.

The weight of doubt, a fleeting glance,
In every flutter, lies a chance.
With wings of hope, we learn to glide,
The heart's true song, our faithful guide.

When doubts dissolve like mist at dawn,
A newfound strength, we venture on.
In every heart, the promise glows,
In feathered grace, our courage grows.

Wrapped in Steel and Ethereal Mist

Wrapped in steel, yet lost in dreams,
We dance in shadows, light's soft gleams.
With hearts of valor, minds set free,
In ethereal mist, we find our key.

In every clash, our spirits rise,
Beyond the veil, where truth belies.
The dawn awaits with arms outstretched,
Through mist and steel, we are enmeshed.

Together strong, through trials we roam,
In unity, we find our home.
What once was lost, we claim anew,
With courage born, our hearts imbue.

Under the Eye of Celestial Watchers

Beneath the vast, unyielding sky,
Stars whisper secrets, winged dreams fly.
A tapestry of fate is spun,
In the dark is where we run.

Winds carry tales from ancient lore,
Echoed softly on the shore.
Moonlight dances on the lake,
Awakens all that dreams awake.

Realm of shadows, bright and bold,
Mysteries in silence fold.
With each heartbeat, the night unfolds,
Stories lost, yet to be told.

Through branches bare, a sigh is heard,
A fragile hope, yet undeterred.
Celestial watchers, eyes alight,
Guide our paths through endless night.

From heights above, their gaze descends,
On weary souls, their warmth extends.
In the quiet, promise sways,
Under skies of endless days.

The Dance of Dusk and Tethered Light

As twilight drapes the world in gold,
Hearts entwined, yet tales unfold.
Fleeting moments weave the air,
In the stillness, dreams we share.

Beneath the boughs, shadows weave,
A dance of light, we dare believe.
Each flicker bright, a moment clasped,
In the night's embrace, we gasp.

Time slows down as colors blend,
Wishing this night would not end.
With every step, our spirits soar,
Tethered light begs for encore.

Voices mingle in a gentle tune,
Under the watch of a crescent moon.
Stars polished in the dusk's embrace,
Every heartbeat finds its place.

So let the dusk my soul ignite,
In the shadows, I find light.
A fleeting dance, yet ever bright,
In memory, we'll hold this night.

Melodies Encased in Shadows of Sorrow

In quiet corners, echoes weep,
Melodies buried, secrets deep.
Whispers linger in the air,
Sadness wrapped in every prayer.

Each note a tear, a silent cry,
Yearning hearts that ache and sigh.
In twilight's grasp, dreams take flight,
Hushed shadows guard the night.

Lost in time, the haunting sound,
Of memory where grief is found.
Yet in sorrow, strength can grow,
A hidden beauty in the woe.

With every chord, the past returns,
A flickering flame, forever burns.
In darkness, we find our grace,
Longing for a warm embrace.

So sing the songs of yesteryears,
In shadows wrapped, through silent tears.
For in the heart, where love resides,
Melodies bloom, and pain subsides.

The Anvil of Dreams and Delusions

In the forge where hopes take flight,
Molded by shadows, kissed with light.
Whispers of courage clash and play,
Beneath the hammer, futures sway.

Hands of fate in iron throng,
Sculpting legacy, righting wrong.
A spark ignites, a fire sings,
While silence weaves what courage brings.

Upon the anvil, wishes burn,
The echoes dance, the pages turn.
In strands of fate, dreams intertwine,
Dancing like flames on a twisted line.

Yet delusions creep, elusive, sly,
Filling the heart with a bitter cry.
Tread carefully on paths you choose,
For in the fire, it's easy to lose.

But still we brave the molten flow,
Crafting from chaos, learning to grow.
In the heat of struggle, hope prevails,
For each dream forged, a tale unveils.

Beneath the Gale's Shadowed Path

In whispers where the wild winds play,
Secrets hide from light of day.
Beneath the gale's breath, shadows chase,
A twisting maze, a hidden place.

Trees bow low as tempests rise,
Lost in the murmurs of ancient skies.
Through brambles and whispers, wanderers tread,
On paths uncharted, where fears are shed.

Yet hope remains, a flickering flame,
Guiding each heart, calling each name.
With courage stout, we brave the storm,
In shadows deep, our spirits warm.

While echoes linger of whispered plight,
The stars reveal their guiding light.
Together we stride, hand in hand,
Chasing dreams on this rugged land.

So let the gale sweep, let it howl,
We'll sing our song, we won't cower,
For every gust and bitter breath,
Leads us onward, defying death.

The Weaving of Stone and Sinew

With hands calloused, a heart of fire,
We weave our tales, lift souls higher.
In stone and sinew, the past entwines,
In threads of fleeting, timeless signs.

Each stitch a story, rich and bold,
Woven with courage, a tapestry told.
Through trials faced, our spirits soar,
Building the bridges to distant shore.

Among the stones, memories lie
Of hopes and dreams that touch the sky.
With every twist and gentle seam,
We craft a future born of dream.

In the weaver's world, all lives connect,
Threads of fate, we can't neglect.
A circle forming, hand in hand,
Together we rise, together we stand.

So let us gather, souls akin,
With faith unyielding, we begin.
The weaving of lives, in harmony bound,
A masterpiece of love profound.

The Hold of Fate's Relentless Grasp

In the stillness where destinies meet,
The grasp of fate is cold and sweet.
With every choice, it pulls us tight,
Dancing shadows in the pale moonlight.

Threads of time in hands unseen,
Woven with care, both harsh and keen.
Through every trial, the heart must learn,
Fate's fire kindles, for passions burn.

Yet fear not the hold, embrace the bind,
For in its grip, we seek and find.
With every heartbeat tethered close,
Hope whispers softly, we must engross.

In the web of time, our paths converge,
With love and strength, we start to surge.
Bound by the stars, we forge ahead,
Through every tear, a thread is spread.

So let us venture, brave the clasp,
With courage fierce and hearts that grasp.
For in this journey, together we'll tread,
In the hold of fate, our hearts are fed.

Ensnared by a Roaring Mystery

In shadows deep, where whispers creep,
A siren's call, a secret to keep.
The forest breathes with ancient sighs,
Beneath the stars, the truth lies.

Fog weaves tales of forgotten lore,
Of brave young hearts who sought much more.
They danced with fate, on perilous ground,
In silence, mysteries abound.

With each step taken, echoes swell,
Of laughter lost and the tolling bell.
In moonlit nights, fear takes flight,
Binding souls 'neath the cloak of night.

A roaring beast, the heart does race,
In untamed wild, we find our place.
Together we chase the dreams untold,
As the mystery enfolds us bold.

So tread with care, oh heart so brave,
For in the dark, the past may wave.
With courage firm and spirit free,
We unlock the chains of history.

The Veil of Nature's Clutch

Beneath the boughs of emerald hue,
Where secrets hide and rumors brew.
A soft caress of dew-kissed morn,
The veil of nature, richly worn.

Whispers croon in the cooling shade,
Of ancient trees, in silence laid.
The roots entwine in a sacred dance,
As time slips softly into trance.

In rustling leaves, a lullaby,
A plea to those who wander nigh.
To seek the magic, wild and pure,
In nature's heart, our spirits cure.

With gentle hands and open eyes,
We find the world in vast disguise.
The clutch of nature, fierce yet kind,
Offers solace for the seeking mind.

So linger here, in golden light,
Let worries fade, drift out of sight.
For within this realm, both calm and lush,
We find our peace in nature's hush.

Where Iron Meets the Fauna's Arm

In places rough where shadows play,
Iron and earth converge in fray.
A clash of worlds, both strong and wild,
Where nature weeps, yet remains beguiled.

With fangs of steel and tender paws,
The dance of fate, and nature's laws.
In the forge's breath, creation wakes,
While life and metal, a bond it makes.

The humming wheels and rusted dreams,
Craft tales of hope in whispered themes.
For in the clash of might and grace,
Beauty blooms in the harshest place.

A world transformed by hands of men,
Yet still, the wild beckons again.
In metal whispers, the wild heart calls,
As iron binds, the spirit enthralls.

So heed the tale, where both can thrive,
In the heart of chaos, we come alive.
Harmony hums, as worlds collide,
Where iron meets the fauna's pride.

Flights of Fancy and Fear

In realms where dreams dare take their flight,
Imagination dances in the night.
With wings of hope and shadows near,
We soar above our whispered fear.

Beneath the clouds, a canvas spreads,
Painting wishes where the heart treads.
Each fantasy, a fleeting spark,
Guiding us through the endless dark.

Yet in the midst of joy's bright chase,
Lies the cold grip of fear's embrace.
For every joy, a price must pay,
A balance found in night and day.

With heart alight, we face the storm,
In swirling doubt, our spirits warm.
Thus side by side, both fancy and dread,
Together we march on threads we tread.

So let us revel in the fray,
For dreams and fears lead the way.
In harmony, they sing their song,
In flights of fancy, we belong.

Threads of Fate Under Watchful Wings

In shadows cast by olden trees,
A whisper weaves through twilight's breeze.
Threads of fate entwined so fine,
Under watchful wings, they shine.

Moonlight dances on the creek,
Secrets hidden, yet they speak.
Carved in bark, the stories lie,
Beneath the vast, unyielding sky.

Echoes of the nightingale,
Through rustling leaves, a gentle tale.
Promises of dawn not far,
Written in the morning star.

Wings of destiny take flight,
Guiding hearts through darkened night.
Each feather tells a woven fate,
In quiet moments, we create.

With starlit paths that intertwine,
In realms where dreams and hopes align.
Threads of life's great tapestry,
Bound together, you and me.

Beneath the Weight of Ancient Feathers

Upon the stones where shadows rest,
Ancient feathers, they attest.
Guardians of lore, they watch and wait,
Beneath the weight of timeless fate.

Amidst the echoes, wisdom flows,
From ashes past, a river grows.
In silent trust, the heart will learn,
To cherish every twist and turn.

The forest whispers tales of old,
In hues of red and glints of gold.
Beneath the boughs, the secrets lay,
Awaiting moments to convey.

With every wingbeat, stories rise,
In twilight's glow, beneath the skies.
The past will guide the steps we tread,
Our destinies in words unsaid.

So listen close, for nature speaks,
In rustling leaves and babbling creeks.
Beneath the weight, we find our grace,
In every thought, in every space.

The Rustle of Hidden Talons

In the stillness of the night,
A sound emerges, soft yet slight.
The rustle of hidden talons near,
Promising truths that draw us here.

In the moon's embrace, shadows creep,
Secrets of the forest keep.
With silent grace, they wander bold,
Tales of wonder yet untold.

Beneath the cloak of stars' bright glow,
Mysterious paths begin to flow.
Each whispered sigh, each fleeting glance,
Awakens dreams in a celestial dance.

Footsteps follow, silent and keen,
In nature's heart, a world unseen.
Through twisted branches, wonders hide,
Where hopes and fears both coincide.

So heed the call of dusk's embrace,
In darkened woods, we find our place.
The rustle beckons, faint yet clear,
To embrace the magic waiting here.

Intertwined Dreams of Stone and Sky

Upon the cliffs where eagles soar,
Intertwined dreams whisper evermore.
Stone and sky in a dance divine,
A tapestry of stars that shine.

The mountains hold the tales of time,
In every crevice, every climb.
Voices echo through the gale,
In nature's ballad, we prevail.

Beneath the arching heavens vast,
Future and present blend at last.
In every heartbeat, every sigh,
Lives entwined where dreams fly high.

Through cragged paths and softest glades,
Wonders bloom in hidden shades.
Weaving together the earth and air,
In unity, we find the rare.

With every breath, we touch the light,
Chasing shadows in the night.
Intertwined, our fates align,
In dreams of stone and sky, we shine.

Fables of the Forgotten Winged Wards

In shadows deep where secrets dwell,
The winged wards weave a silent spell.
With feathers bright as dawn's first light,
They guard the dreams of the lost in night.

Through whispered winds, their stories flow,
Of flights endured and valleys low.
In every flap of a fragile wing,
A memory of hope begins to sing.

Yet time does steal the light away,
Their magic wanes as night turns gray.
The wards once fierce now fade to dreams,
Lost are their songs, or so it seems.

Yet find them still in children's tales,
Of ancient flights o'er moonlit trails.
In hearts where wonder never dies,
The winged wards live, in softest sighs.

Threads of Twilight in Iron's Embrace

From forges deep where shadows play,
The iron threads weave night and day.
In twilight's grasp, strong hands will mold,
The fabric of dreams, both brave and bold.

Each strand a whisper of fate on high,
An echo of laughter, a silent cry.
Through clashing sparks and ember's dance,
The twilight breathes, giving life a chance.

Yet chains can bind what yearns to soar,
In iron's embrace, the heart feels sore.
But twilight weaves its magic still,
In threads of iron, heart meets will.

Rise from the depths, the spirits say,
For every dark, brings light of day.
In twilight's glow, possibilities gleam,
Threads of our lives, the fabric of dream.

Intertwined Whispers of Wood and Wind

In ancient groves where secrets lie,
The wood and wind in concert sigh.
With roots that reach both deep and wide,
They cradle stories, where spirits bide.

Leaves dance gently, in threes or twos,
Sharing tales of the morning dew.
As branches sway, in whispers blend,
The wood and wind, they often mend.

Yet storms will come and tempests roar,
Breaking bonds that were once rapport.
But through the chaos, life renews,
In wood and wind, strength imbues.

So listen close to the whispers sweet,
For nature's song is a wondrous feat.
Intertwined, they craft our fate,
In every sigh, a world awaits.

A Lament for the Wingless Wanderers

In shadows cast where silence clings,
The wingless wanderers mourn their wings.
With aching hearts, they roam the ground,
In search of skies, but never found.

Each step a tale of hopes displaced,
In every glance, a dream embraced.
Longing for heights they'll never see,
A burden borne, yet spirits free.

The songs of flight ring in their ears,
Through endless nights and hidden tears.
Yet still they wander, brave and bold,
In tales of courage, their hearts unfold.

A lament shared with the moonlit night,
For every wanderer lost from flight.
Though grounded here, their dreams take soar,
The wingless remain, forevermore.

The Roots Interlaced with Aether

Beneath the ancient oaks they lie,
Roots entwined with secrets nigh.
Whispers of the earth's soft song,
Echoes where the shadows throng.

Glimmers of the stars above,
Woven threads of earth and love.
Crimson vines and silver dew,
Dance beneath the sky so blue.

When twilight paints the world in gray,
The roots reach out, they gently sway.
In dreams of leafy canopies,
The aether sings of mysteries.

Within the soil, the magic stirs,
As time flows like the whispered purrs.
A harmony of life unfurled,
In every corner of this world.

So wander close and close your eyes,
To feel the pulse that never lies.
For nature's heart, it beats with grace,
In every root, in every space.

Caged Visions in Cerulean Shadows

In corners dim where dreams take flight,
Visions flicker in fading light.
Cerulean shadows stretch and yawn,
While secrets whisper, softly drawn.

Caged within a fragile frame,
They dance and flutter, wild yet tame.
Each thought, a bird on twilight's wing,
Chasing echoes of what they sing.

The night enfolds them in its cloak,
As silent wishes softly smoke.
With every wish, a shiver grown,
Among the stars, they're never alone.

Desires nourish, like rain on seed,
In silent worlds where hearts take heed.
From shadows deep, the light will break,
To weave the dreams our souls awake.

So linger long in twilight's hue,
For visions wait and hope renew.
In cages close, they'll stretch and soar,
In cerulean shadows, evermore.

The Veil of Silent Wings

A hush descends upon the night,
As stars emerge in pure delight.
In the stillness, time stands still,
A moment held by nature's will.

The veil between the worlds, so thin,
Where whispers blend and dreams begin.
Silent wings that brush the air,
Carrying secrets, light as prayer.

Through silver clouds, they glide with grace,
Unseen dancers in this place.
With every beat, the night unfolds,
A tapestry of tales untold.

Here, shadows merge with dawn's first light,
In the peace of the coming night.
The veil lifts softly, secrets shared,
In the warmth of love that's dared.

So close your eyes and feel the care,
Of silent wings that linger there.
For in their flight, a truth awaits,
Within the veil, love never fades.

Nurtured in Grasp of Clay and Flight

In gentle hands, the clay is formed,
A vessel shaped, the heart warmed.
Each curve brings life, each line a fate,
Where dreams reside, and hopes await.

From earth we rise, to skies we soar,
Nurtured roots, forevermore.
In vibrant hues, the blossoms grow,
A dance of life, a wondrous show.

So cast your gaze to heights unknown,
Where seeds of thought are freely sown.
With every breath, the journey starts,
The clay of life, the flight of hearts.

Through trials fierce and tempests bold,
In stories woven, tales unfold.
Within the grasp of earth and air,
Our spirits learn what dreams may dare.

To fly, to bloom, to find our way,
In grounded strength, we seize the day.
For nurtured in the grasp so tight,
We rise as one, in shared flight.

The Binding of The Skyward Heart

In the quiet dusk, a whisper flies,
Above the trees, where the dreaming lies.
Hearts entwined in a silken thread,
Bound by wishes that softly spread.

Stars awaken in the night's embrace,
Casting shadows with a gentle grace.
The moonlight dances, a waltz so bright,
Guiding lost souls through the velvet night.

From ancient tales, the echoes call,
Every heartbeat a promise to enthrall.
Each breath a wish that the heavens hear,
A melody sweet, wrapped in hope and fear.

In the woven tapestry of fate,
Every moment is gentle, yet great.
With every heartbeat, the sky unfolds,
A story of love that forever holds.

So let the skyward heart combine,
In realms where dreams and starlight shine.
Together, they'll rise, uncovering the part,
Of the binding love in the skyward heart.

Tethered upon the Apex of Fear

At the peak where shadows intertwine,
Fear whispers secrets, both bitter and fine.
A tether of doubt wraps tight around,
In the clutch of silence, no solace found.

Yet within the fog, a flicker of light,
A courage that stands, ready to fight.
To rise above what the heart does dread,
And hold onto dreams, though they seem dead.

With trembling hands, the edge looks near,
But bravery blooms in the face of fear.
Like fragile vines that reach for the sky,
They cling to the hope, refusing to die.

So take a breath, let the courage soar,
For on the edge, there's so much more.
Beyond the fear, the unknown awaits,
A journey begun, as destiny fates.

Tethered yet strong, the spirit will break,
Through the boundless dark, for the future's sake.
And when fear's grip fades thin and clear,
The apex will shine—hold on, my dear.

The Flightless Echoes of Destiny

In the hollow of dreams, the echoes play,
Whispers of fate in the light of day.
With wings unseen, they flutter and sigh,
Tracing the paths where the lost ones lie.

Flightless and free, their spirits remain,
Carrying burdens of joy and pain.
In the quiet murmurs of the heart's own tune,
They dance with shadows beneath the moon.

Each choice we make, a thread finely spun,
In the tapestry bright where the stories run.
Although they may falter, these echoes will rise,
Finding their way through the darkest skies.

Destiny calls with a voice ever true,
In the hearts of those who believe anew.
Though flightless they seem, they carry the spark,
Of a journey begun in the depths of the dark.

So listen closely to what they proclaim,
For flightless echoes still whisper your name.
In the still of the night, let your spirit be free,
Embrace every echo; they lead you to be.

The Lonesome Garden of Woven Fates

In a garden where shadows softly creep,
Petals of time lie in twilight steep.
Each bloom a moment, each thorn a tale,
Of woven fates where the heart can ail.

Whispers of nature coax secrets to share,
In the lonesome garden where few dare to care.
Yet beauty abounds, though the path be rough,
Resilience grows where the soil is tough.

With every step, the memories hum,
A symphony played on a heartstring's drum.
Though lonesome it seems, there's friendship in pain,
In the quiet embrace of the gentle rain.

So nurture the garden with love and grace,
For every loss, it finds its place.
The lonesome blooms will still weave their art,
Reminding the soul that all beings are part.

In the tapestry rich, where fate intertwines,
The garden of fate grows resilient vines.
So walk through the gloom, let your spirit elate,
In the lonesome garden of woven fate.

Shattered Dreams Held Firmly Close

In the quiet of the night, they weep,
Fleeting visions fade into deep.
Whispers echo in the shadows' glow,
A tapestry of hopes laid low.

Yet hearts clutch to fragments, dear,
Each memory held, even in fear.
For within the ashes, embers flicker,
A promise lingers, soft and thicker.

With every dawn, the light will break,
A chance to heal, a path to stake.
And dreams, though shattered, find their way,
In fragile arcs to greet the day.

So stand and face the stormy blast,
With courage drawn from lessons passed.
For in the struggle, beauty grows,
Through shattered dreams held warmly close.

The Cradle of Wings in Tightly Coiled Threads

In the corner of a world unseen,
Where shadows dance with fleeting sheen.
A cradle swings on threads so frail,
Holding secrets in a whispered trail.

With wings of gossamer, they dare,
To lift the lost from dreamer's air.
In tightly coiled, they find their grace,
As stardust weaves a timeless space.

Each heartbeat thrums with ancient song,
Echoes where forgotten belong.
In the cradle, a flicker of flight,
A journey born in soft twilight.

For those who linger in the dark,
May find the spark, a lasting mark.
With every flutter, hope ascends,
In tightly coiled threads, a world mends.

The Silken Bonds of Forgotten Whispers

In twilight's hush, secrets play,
Silken bonds weave night from day.
Forgotten whispers cling like dew,
Stories spun from long ago, too.

With each soft thread, they intertwine,
A tapestry of wishes fine.
In shadows cast by moons and stars,
They cradle hearts, they mend the scars.

But echoes lost in silence tread,
Like fragile dreams that must be fed.
A sigh, a laugh, they float in air,
A promise made, a truth laid bare.

Through winding paths of chance and fate,
The silken bonds, they resonate.
In every fiber, love persists,
A wish upon a moonlit mist.

Ties to the Ethereal Clamor

In shadows where the silence breaks,
A world awakens, trembles, shakes.
Ties to the ethereal clamor sing,
As spirits dance on feathered wing.

Through misty veils, they sway and sway,
Guiding lost hearts along their way.
In whispers soft, the night implores,
Unlock the dreams behind closed doors.

With every note, a tale unfolds,
Of love and loss, of dreams retold.
The stars bear witness to the light,
In the clamor of the endless night.

So heed the call of distant grace,
In every shadow, find your place.
For ties to the ethereal clamor grow,
A symphony of all we know.

The Echo of Silent Tethers

In the stillness where shadows creep,
Dreams take flight, yet secrets keep.
The heartstrings hum a solemn tune,
Beneath the watchful gaze of moon.

Whispers stir in the quiet night,
Threads that bind, both soft and tight.
Memories linger, sweet and dear,
Echoes of voices we long to hear.

In the depths, shadows softly play,
Reminders of love that fades away.
In the silence, tethers draw near,
Connecting souls that still hold dear.

Each heartbeat echoes past regrets,
In the twilight where darkness sets.
Yet hope remains, a glimmer bright,
Illuminating the endless night.

Through the stillness, we find our light,
In every tether, a spark of fight.
For love endures, though miles apart,
A timeless bond, the silent heart.

Shadows of Flight and Resolve

Beneath the clouds, the phoenix soars,
A dance of shadows, a tale of wars.
With wings of fire, it cuts the sky,
In search of dreams that never die.

Through twilight's haze, the echoes call,
Courage born from knowing the fall.
In every heartbeat, strength is found,
In silent vows that know no bound.

As shadows stretch, the night unfolds,
A story whispered, a fate foretold.
In the darkness, resolve takes flight,
Chasing the stars that pierce the night.

With every flap, a hope ignites,
A glimmer seen in the darkest nights.
For shadows teach, and shadows guide,
In flight, we learn to brave the tide.

In this journey, the heart finds peace,
A melody that will never cease.
With every shadow, a tale to weave,
In the dance of hope, we believe.

Whispers Within the Iron Grip

In the clutch of shadows broad and deep,
Whispers linger where memories sleep.
Iron grips the dreams once bright,
Yet in the dark, we still find light.

Through the corridors of time and pain,
The heart resilient, yet bound in chain.
Whispers call from a distant shore,
A gentle tug, a knock at the door.

Beneath the surface, a fire brews,
Stories of hope tangled in clues.
Each whisper softens the iron's hold,
Turning the silent into the bold.

In the struggle, a fierce embrace,
In the depths, we find our place.
With whispered truths and shadows drawn,
We rise anew with every dawn.

Though iron grips may seek to bind,
The whispers echo, gentle yet kind.
In each heart, a spirit ignites,
Unfurling wings, ready for flights.

The Dance of Oak and Feather

In the glade where whispers dwell,
Oak and feather weave a spell.
Roots run deep, while branches sway,
In the dance of night and day.

A feather drifts on the breeze of time,
Carrying secrets, lost in rhyme.
While oaken strength anchors the ground,
Together they sing, a bond profound.

Underneath the starlit skies,
The dance unravels, no goodbyes.
With every gust, new stories played,
In harmony, nature's serenade.

From the depths, a wisdom grows,
In the rustle where the wild wind blows.
For in the dance of oak and plume,
We find a heart that can resume.

As seasons turn and time bestows,
The dance continues, while the river flows.
In unity, we find our grace,
In the dance of feathered embrace.

The Riddles of Earthbound Aspirations

In shadows cast by hopes yet bold,
A whisper rides the winds of gold.
Each dream a seed in twilight sown,
To bloom where heartbeats find their home.

The earth beneath, a canvas wide,
With paths of stone and stars beside.
Yet tangled roots may bind the brave,
For fortune's smile is seldom paved.

A chain of choices in the dust,
In every fall, a rise is thrust.
As echoes dance through time undone,
We quest for light, our battles won.

But riddles lie in laughter's wake,
In every choice, a world to make.
And so we fetch our dreams anew,
For earthbound wishes fly like dew.

With every turn, a tale to weave,
In spiraled paths, we dare believe.
For in the heart of silent night,
The riddle hums in soft twilight.

Skyward Longing Beneath Mutable Grasp

Beneath the arch of twilight's veil,
The stars emerge with whispered tales.
Each shimmer speaks of journeys far,
While souls reach out for twilight's star.

The clouds drift softly, dreams take flight,
In pondered thoughts of day and night.
But hands that stretch to catch the gleam,
Find fleeting wishes like a dream.

A secret yearning in the breeze,
As memories dance among the trees.
The skies reflect our hearts' designs,
In every quest for love that shines.

Yet shadows wander, doubts may rise,
While moments fade like whispered sighs.
But hope ignites with every dawn,
A testament to dreams reborn.

So let us rise on winds that flow,
With hearts entwined, through pain and glow.
For skyward longing's gentle clasp,
In every heart, a dream to grasp.

Poised Between Rooftop and Dream

On rooftops high where echoes play,
A world unfolds in shades of gray.
With hearts alight and spirits free,
We dance on ledges, you and me.

The city sprawls like tales untold,
In every corner, lives unfold.
Yet here we stand, in twilight's grace,
Our laughter finding sacred space.

With eyes aglow, the stars ignite,
In whispered dreams that paint the night.
But fear may coil in shadows deep,
As secrets threaten stillness' keep.

Yet poised we are, on edges fine,
With every heartbeat, dreams align.
For in the balance, courage lies,
In laughter sweet, the spirit flies.

So let us breath this evening's air,
With every thought, a silent prayer.
On rooftops high, we weave our schemes,
Between the world and waking dreams.

The Order of the Tethered Spirits

In circles wide, a bond is drawn,
With whispers shared at break of dawn.
Each spirit tethered, wild and free,
In unity, a tapestry.

We gather close, a silent pact,
As echoes swirl in memories backed.
In laughter's light, the shadows fade,
With love unchained and courage laid.

Yet trials rise like storms at sea,
As doubts may gnaw at destiny.
But through the tempest, hearts will soar,
For tethered souls will seek for more.

With every story, strength is found,
In bonds that hold on hallowed ground.
An order forged in night's embrace,
Where every spirit finds its place.

So let us raise our voices high,
With echoes caught in twilight's sigh.
For every spirit linked in trust,
In boundless dreams, we rise, we must.

The Grip of Time and Terra

In the whisper of the ancient trees,
The seconds dance like autumn leaves.
Each moment holds a quiet lore,
Binding earth and sky, forevermore.

As shadows stretch, they weave and merge,
The pulse of time begins to surge.
With every heartbeat, stories climb,
The endless grip of time and terra rhyme.

O'er mountains tall and rivers wide,
With gentle hands, the ages bide.
The thread of fate, so finely spun,
As seasons chase, and dreams outrun.

In twilight's glow, the echoes fade,
While starlit paths are softly laid.
Yet in the dark, hope softly glows,
A promise in the earth, it sows.

Through every hour, the sand does flow,
In cycles vast, the past will grow.
Yet still, we stand, with hearts entwined,
In the grip of time, our souls aligned.

Shadows Cradle the Sundered Dream

In the stillness of a moonlit night,
Whispers dance in the silver light.
A fractured dream, with edges blurred,
In shadows deep, all hope deferred.

The secrets held by moonbeams pale,
Guide the lost through the haunted veil.
Each echo calls with a soft despair,
While shadows cradle the dreams laid bare.

With ink-stained skies and hearts adrift,
We search for solace, a fragile gift.
Yet in the dark, connections gleam,
As light creeps softly into the dream.

The night reveals both pain and grace,
In every tear, a tender trace.
Though paths are twisted, the stars align,
For every heart, a thread divine.

As dawn approaches, hope will rise,
Casting away the shadowed lies.
And in the light, our dreams will bloom,
No longer bound to silent gloom.

The Chained Heart's Requiem

In the quiet of a heartbeat's pause,
Chains formed strong from life's deep flaws.
A heart once bold, now wrapped in fear,
Yet still, it longs for what is near.

Within the cage of iron might,
The whispers wane in grateful light.
A requiem for dreams once bright,
As shadows fall, it takes to flight.

Each link a memory, forged in pain,
Yet freedom sings in soft refrain.
With every tear, a tale unfolds,
The strength of love cannot be sold.

Through endless night, a flicker glows,
A sign of hope where courage grows.
The chains may cling, but love's embrace,
Will guide the heart to open space.

With every beat, a pact is made,
To rise again from anguish laid.
For in the depths, true strength will find,
The chained heart's path, forever kind.

A Tapestry of Wings and Bonds

In the realm where the starlings sing,
Threads of fate weave a mighty wing.
With every twist, a tale unfolds,
In colors bright, the story holds.

Wings extend, in freedom's grace,
Boundless dreams in this sacred space.
Each bond a knot, so carefully tied,
In the whispers of the winds, we confide.

Through valleys deep and mountains high,
Our spirits soar 'neath the endless sky.
Each journey shared, a vibrant hue,
A tapestry of me and you.

With every flutter, hope takes flight,
In shadows cast by the setting light.
The world unfolds, a grand delight,
As hearts entwine, our souls ignite.

For in the tapestry, love forever dwells,
A symphony of stories that time compels.
With wings spread wide, ready to soar,
In bonds we share, we find our core.

A Song for the Bound and Forgotten

In shadows deep where whispers creep,
The lost souls sigh in moonlight's keep.
Their dreams once bright like stars above,
Now flicker dim, devoid of love.

With chains that bind, they wander low,
Through fields of time with naught to show.
Yet hope may spark within the heart,
To light the way, a brand new start.

On paths of dust and forgotten tales,
Their voices rise like distant wails.
Through forgotten doors, they seek the key,
For freedom's call shall set them free.

The wind may carry their names in spite,
A ballad born of endless night.
And echoes sing of courage bold,
In every heart, a truth retold.

So raise a glass to those unseen,
Who journey onward, brave and keen.
Their songs will linger in the air,
A melody of loss and care.

The Resilience of Steel and Air

Beneath the weight of time and toil,
The forge ignites as spirits coil.
With every strike, resilience found,
In steel and air, the heart unbound.

Through smoke and fire, the metal bends,
The essence of a dream descends.
A symphony of clash and flame,
In every spark, a silent name.

The hammer's dance, a skilled ballet,
Crafting strength in night and day.
For in the heat, the truth is cast,
A legacy of futures vast.

With every piece, a tale is spun,
Of battles fought, and victories won.
In every link, a story weaves,
Of souls that dared and hearts that believe.

The skies may roar, the winds may howl,
But steadfast dreams in metal scowl.
With every breath, resilience grows,
In steel and air, the courage flows.

Sidle of the Silent Watcher

In twilight's haze, a figure stands,
With knowing eyes and open hands.
A silent watcher, wise and true,
With tales of starlight, soft and blue.

Through glades of green and fields of gold,
The whispers of ancient nights unfold.
With every breeze, a memory fades,
In shadows cast by forest glades.

What stories linger in those eyes?
What secrets sleep beneath the skies?
Patience carved by the years' embrace,
In silence holds a sacred space.

As echoes drift on silvered streams,
And shimmer softly into dreams.
The watcher waits, with heart aglow,
In quietude, the world will grow.

For wisdom dwells in softest tones,
In silence shared, the heart atones.
Let those who know the stillness see,
The beauty in the mystery.

Secrets Tied in a Forgotten Grasp

In dusty tomes where shadows dwell,
Lies woven secrets none can tell.
Forgotten hands, they trace the lines,
Of ancient lore, of lost designs.

With every page, a world unveiled,
Of heroes bold and hope curtailed.
In whispered tones, the stories fold,
A tapestry of dreams retold.

Through tangled roots of time's embrace,
The secrets hide, a hidden place.
Each sigh of history, bound in ink,
Awaits the touch, the fated link.

What truths await the daring heart,
To pry the past and make a start?
Each thread a path through night's regale,
A quest for those who dare unveil.

So let us grasp what once was lost,
And venture forth, no matter cost.
For in the darkness, light we find,
As secrets sing and hearts unwind.

Whispers of the Birdsong Iron

In the heart of the night, a soft tune swells,
Notes like starlight, in shadows, they dwell.
Glistening dreams in the dew-kissed air,
Secrets of nature, laid tender and rare.

Flutters of magic, on wings they soar,
Glimpses of wonder, forevermore.
Each whisper a promise, a tale to be spun,
A song of the forest, where all has begun.

Murmurs of wisdom, an ancient refrain,
Binding the wild, through joy and through pain.
In harmony woven, they dance through the trees,
Life's gentle chorus, afloat on the breeze.

When twilight descends, in silver and gold,
The tales of the birdies, in starlight retold.
With every sweet note, the world comes alive,
In whispers of song, the heart learns to thrive.

So heed well the notes, the beauty they bring,
In the whispers of birds, the joy of the spring.
For as long as they sing, through the night and the dawn,
A tapestry woven, the magic lives on.

Shadows in the Grasp of Fate

Beneath the heavy sky, where shadows scheme,
Fates intertwine, like threads in a dream.
Each step a whisper, each glance a thread,
Caught in the web where the brave fear to tread.

A dance of illusions, the light and the dark,
In the heart of the chaos, the flickering spark.
Time swirls like smoke, in the stillness, it waits,
Chasing the echoes of your tangled fates.

The moon sheds its tears, on the edges of night,
Guiding the lost with its silvery light.
While shadows are dancing, they beckon so sly,
A lure to the heart that dares to comply.

In the silence, there's power, in quiet resolve,
Facing the shadows, the secrets they solve.
As dawn breaks with courage, in colors so bright,
Shadows dissolve, in the glow of the light.

So walk with your heart in the clasp of the night,
Embrace all the trials, and summon your might.
For fate may be fickle, but you hold the key,
In the dance of the shadows, find the courage to be.

The Grip of Sable Wings

In the hush of the night, where secrets conspire,
Sable wings whisper, igniting desire.
Veils of the cosmos, in silence they glide,
Carrying dreams on the wings of the tide.

Eyes like the stars, a gaze that can pierce,
Drawing you closer, the heartbeats, they hear.
In shadows they linger, with elegance and grace,
A reminder of beauty in an endless race.

The stillness of night wraps around like a cloak,
Embracing the whispers of promise they spoke.
On the edge of the darkness, where night takes its toll,
The grip of sable wings cradles the soul.

With the flutter of feathers, a dance softly blooms,
In corners of twilight, dispelling the glooms.
With every soft caress, they weave paths anew,
Threads of enchantment in shadows they strew.

So surrender to wonder, let your spirit take flight,
In the grasp of the sable, find solace in night.
For dreams are the wings that set hearts aglow,
In the dark's gentle embrace, let your true self show.

Echoes of the Silent Forest

In the depths of the woods, where the ancients reside,
Echoes of stories in silence they bide.
Whispers of wisdom, in shadows concealed,
Each rustle and sigh, a secret revealed.

Underneath canopies, of moss and of pine,
Nature's soft heartbeat, a rhythm divine.
In the dappled sunlight, the spirits glide near,
Carrying legends for the ones who will hear.

The breeze hums a tune, like a lullaby sung,
Awakening echoes of old while we're young.
Through bark and through branches, the stories intertwine,

A dance of connection, by fate's grand design.

Among the shadows, a stillness is found,
Grounded in moments where magic abounds.
The trees stand as giants, in silence they speak,
Guardians of secrets, to those who will seek.

So wander the pathways, let your spirit roam free,
In the echoes of silence, discover the key.
For the forest has tales, as deep as the sea,
In its whispers and rustles, find who you may be.

The Confluence of Time and Talon

In twilight's embrace, shadows entwine,
Where whispers of ages in dusk do align.
Wings brush the air, silent yet bold,
As time's flowing river reveals tales untold.

Stars flicker softly, a dance in the night,
A tapestry woven with threads of pure light.
Through the branches, the wind sings a tune,
While secrets are kept beneath the pale moon.

Ancient stones murmur, each heartbeat a lore,
Of those who have soared, and those who implore.
Their echoes resound in the hearts of the wise,
Where dreams take to flight, like sparks in the skies.

In this sacred space where the moments converge,
Dreamers and doers feel power emerge.
A talon grips tightly, yet yearns to let go,
In the confluence of time, where rivers do flow.

So listen intently to the night's gentle plea,
For in every heartbeat, a story shall be.
With courage ignited and futures embraced,
Together we travel, where time is interlaced.

Gnarled Roots and Feathers Alight

In the heart of the woods, where shadows renew,
Gnarled roots twist like thoughts, dense and askew.
Beneath rustling leaves, a feather takes flight,
A promise of hope in the longening night.

Whispers of nature breathe life into stone,
Each branch a connection, each moss a bone.
The old trees stand guard, their stories unfold,
While secrets are cradled in whispers of gold.

Feathers alight on the spellbinding air,
Like wishes that flutter though all depths of despair.
They dance through the twilight, a sign of the free,
In the gnarled embrace of what once used to be.

Roots deep and ancient entwine every dream,
Yet lift us in flight as if caught in a beam.
With softness and strength, they teach us to grow,
In this tapestry woven, we're never alone.

So take to the skies, let the heart guide the way,
Through the fibers of time, where wishes will sway.
For each feather that falls holds a tale of its own,
In the echo of roots, we find our true home.

The Burden of the Unyielding Heart

Beneath the hard shell, the heart beats in shade,
A fortress of feelings, a dance yet unplayed.
In silence it waits, unwavering, still,
The burden of dreams, both a whisper and thrill.

With echoes of longing, the heart pushes through,
Each throb a reminder of what's tried and true.
But weight can be heavy when carried alone,
As the tightness of longing turns into a stone.

Yet hope does not falter, nor refuse to ignite,
For deep in the shadows, there lingers a light.
With every soft sigh and each tear that does fall,
The heart slowly learns to embrace, not to stall.

In moments of anguish, a bond may emerge,
With courage as armor, the soul learns to surge.
For the burden, once heavy, may lighten with time,
As the heart, ever brave, begins to unwind.

So cherish the struggles, the battles we fight,
For they carve our essence, like stars in the night.
The unyielding heart, though worn and apart,
Will find strength in the beauty of its fragile art.

Testament of Feather and Forged Bond

In the quiet of morning, where daylight unfolds,
A feather descends, a promise retold.
It dances on breezes with whispers of grace,
A testament born from the heart's gentle space.

Threads of connection, entwined in the air,
Two souls become one, through courage they dare.
With each beat of wings, new paths will align,
In the tapestry woven, where destinies twine.

The bonds forged in fire, together we stand,
With feathers to guide us, and dreams close at hand.
Through storms and through shadows, we rise and we fall,

For strength lies in togetherness, binding us all.

In the dance of the heavens, our spirits take flight,
Illuminated softly by the glow of twilight.
With hearts intertwining, we weather the storms,
A testament living where love truly warms.

So cherish the feathers, the bonds that we share,
For in every heartbeat, there's magic laid bare.
This testament carved in the fabric of time,
Is the essence of love, in rhythm and rhyme.

Caged by the Echoing Roar

In shadows deep, where echoes dwell,
A heart beats loud, creating spell.
Caged in fear, the dreams collide,
With roars that haunt, they cannot hide.

Beneath the weight of silent pleas,
A whisper stirs among the trees.
Through fractured night, hope pushes forth,
Seeking the light, awakening worth.

Walls of metal, rusted and hard,
Yet soft within, a clashing shard.
The echoing roar, it drowns the mind,
Yet courage blooms, no longer confined.

A journey calls from beyond the pin,
Where freedom waits, a new life to win.
With every step, the cage will shake,
And from the past, new paths will break.

So let the echo shape your song,
And forge the fire, where you belong.
In caged despair, let spirits soar,
With whispered hope, unlock the door.

Nocturnal Tales of Woven Strength

In the hush of night, secrets rise,
Beneath the moon's soft, watchful eyes.
A tapestry spun from shadows wide,
Woven with strength that cannot hide.

The stars above twinkle in dreams,
As ancient tales ripple like streams.
With every thread, a story told,
Of bravery forged in nights so cold.

Through tangled paths, the wanderers tread,
With whispers of hope, the lost aren't dead.
In every heart, a spark ignites,
As darkness bends, revealing lights.

The owls call out in haunting tones,
Guiding the weary, the lost souls' drones.
In woven strength, the bonds will hold,
As night unfolds its magic bold.

So gather round, let courage gleam,
In nocturnal tales, we find our dream.
From woven threads, our lives are spun,
In strength united, we are one.

Threads of the Ancient Keeper

In halls of stone where shadows creep,
The ancient keeper guards his sleep.
With threads of time that weave and fray,
He shapes the dawn from yesterday.

The whispers of lost seasons call,
In every echo, a rise and fall.
With patient hands, he spins the tale,
Of joy and sorrow, love's soft veil.

Through whispered dreams and timeless lore,
He stitches fate, forevermore.
Each thread a bond, each knot a tear,
A tapestry of all we share.

In twilight's grasp, the story bends,
As ancient threads find their true ends.
With every twist, a breath of life,
In woven peace, beyond the strife.

So gather close, and heed the call,
For in his hands, we rise or fall.
The ancient keeper's wisdom flows,
And in his care, our journey grows.

Secrets Held by the Feathered Maw

In the forest deep, where shadows play,
Secrets linger in bright array.
The feathered maw keeps quiet still,
Holding whispers of nature's will.

With vibrant wings and piercing gaze,
The guardians watch through misty haze.
A promise made in twilight's hush,
To guide the lost in dawn's soft blush.

Amid the leaves, the stories bloom,
Of lives entwined in fate's sweet loom.
The feathered maw, with secrets spun,
Unfurls the path for everyone.

Through rustling branches, truths take flight,
Illuminating the darkest night.
With every flap, a hope to sow,
In whispered tales, the courage grows.

So heed the call of wings in flight,
For in their secrets lies the light.
The feathered maw shall lead the way,
To brighter tomorrows, day by day.

The Spirits Whisper Beneath the Watcher

In twilight's glow, shadows glint,
Faint echoes call from the thickened mint.
Beneath the gaze of the ancient stone,
Spirits murmur in a hushed tone.

Leaves rustle secrets, softly they weave,
Threads of memory, hearts believe.
With every sigh from the breath of night,
The whispering spirits take their flight.

Moonlight dances on a silver thread,
Guiding lost wanderers where dreams are led.
In truth's embrace, they find their way,
Through timeless realms where shadows play.

With fading light, they weave and twine,
Connections forged where worlds combine.
In the silence, stories are shared,
Through shifting shades, no soul is spared.

So heed the call beneath the moon,
Listen closely for the sweet, soft tune.
For in the stillness, the whispers swell,
And spirits linger where lives compel.

Songs Entangled in Steel and Air

Beneath the clang of hammer's might,
The songs arise in sparks of light.
Entwined with steel, they twist and turn,
Echoes of passion, forever they burn.

In clouds of dust, the notes take flight,
Crafted by hands that bend the night.
Voices mingle in the dance of fate,
A symphony rising to illuminate.

From anvils deep, the melodies soar,
Each strike a promise, an opened door.
The air vibrates with a rhythmic thread,
Where heartbeats strum to the songs unsaid.

Legends forged in shadows of flame,
Each whispering tune carves out a name.
In the realm of the brave, where spirits dare,
Songs entwine in steel and air.

So let the music be your guide,
As you walk beside the river's tide.
For every sound that lingers near,
Melts the boundaries of doubt and fear.

The Pull of Tagetes Under Ancient Stars

Beneath the arc of an endless sky,
The tagetes bloom, where secrets lie.
Golden petals, with earth they sway,
In the dance of night, they find their way.

Ancient stars whisper of tales untold,
Of love and loss, of hearts that bold.
Pulled by the gravity of their light,
Petals shimmer in the soft twilight.

In the garden's heart, hidden truths grow,
With fragrance thick, they ebb and flow.
Each whisper sown in the night's embrace,
Connects the past within sacred space.

A yearning stirs in the moon's soft gaze,
As dreams awaken in a dusky haze.
The tagetes' pull, a magnetic sigh,
Unites the earth with the starlit sky.

So linger beneath this celestial throne,
Where flowers dance, and love is known.
For in their glow, the universe sways,
A cosmic waltz in the night's ballet.

The Unraveling of Forgotten Trysts

In corners dim where shadows blend,
Forgotten trysts begin to mend.
Secrets buried in time's embrace,
Whispers revive in a familiar space.

Threads once tangled now gently fray,
As memories rise from the depths of gray.
Longing rekindles in faintest light,
Two souls entwined through the cloak of night.

With hesitant steps, they trace the ground,
Echoes of laughter in silence found.
The past unravels with every glance,
Their hearts entwined in a timeless dance.

Through veils of mist, their paths align,
In unspoken words, destinies intertwine.
Each heartbeat whispers what dreams have sought,
The unraveling of love, both gained and fought.

So venture forth into the twilight haze,
Where shadows slip into dawn's soft praise.
For in the unravelling of every thread,
Lies the beauty of all that's said and unsaid.

The Art of Constraint in the Wilderness

In the thicket where the wild things grow,
A silent dance, a whispering flow.
Nature's grip, firm yet fair,
Holds the secrets, a breath of air.

Each path chosen, shadows cast,
Like the stories of the past.
With every step, the heart beats loud,
In the wild, away from the crowd.

Branches weave their ancient tales,
As the gentle wind unveils.
In constraints, the freedom lies,
Underneath the endless skies.

With eyes wide open, we behold,
The mysteries that nature told.
Finding joy within the binds,
In the solace that it finds.

Each moment spent in soft embrace,
Is a treasure, a sacred space.
For in the wild, constraints set free,
The wandering spirit's symphony.

Beneath Wings of Primal Majesty

Above the world, so vast and wide,
Majestic wings in graceful glide.
They sweep the skies, a dance of grace,
Beneath their might, we find our place.

In twilight's glow, their shadows fall,
An ancient call, a siren's thrall.
The heartbeat of the land they share,
A bond of breath, a silent prayer.

With feathers kissed by dawn's first light,
They paint the canvas of the night.
In flight, they weave the tales of old,
Stories of courage, fierce and bold.

Each flapping wing holds dreams unsaid,
Of journeys taken, of paths they tread.
Beneath their wings, we rise and soar,
Craving more, forever explore.

For in their flight, we glimpse our fate,
Beneath the stars, we resonate.
In primal majesty, we find,
The wild spirit, intertwined.

When Claws Meet the Shaded Earth

In the hush of twilight's breath,
A dance is born, near life and death.
Claws graze softly, marked in time,
An echo of an ancient rhyme.

Beneath the boughs where shadows play,
Each step whispers the night's ballet.
The earth yields softly, home to dreams,
Where strength meets grace in haunting themes.

Dusk brings forth the hunter's eye,
With stealthy steps, they prowl and fly.
In every rustle, stories blend,
A tapestry that has no end.

When claws meet earth, a pact is made,
In silent woods, the debts are paid.
Respect the balance, heed the call,
For lurking shadows can enthrall.

In primal soil, life's threads entwine,
Where nature's grip is firm yet benign.
The dance of fierce, the calm of peace,
In the shaded earth, all fears cease.

The Looming Shadows of Guardian Creatures

Beneath the moon, where secrets speak,
The guardian creatures softly sneak.
With watchful eyes, they trace the night,
In looming shadows, they take flight.

Forests whisper ancient lore,
Of beings known, and spirits soar.
They guard the paths both wise and worn,
From dusk till dawn, their pledge is sworn.

Each flicker of a candlelight,
Calls forth the magic of the night.
In every rustle, breath holds fast,
With fleeting glimpses of the past.

These shadows may seem dark and cold,
Yet warmth within their hearts unfolds.
For in their watch, protection lies,
A bond that journeys through the skies.

The guardian creatures' silent vow,
To keep the balance, here and now.
In sacred realms where shadows dwell,
Their presence casts a timeless spell.

Emblems of Myth and Ironwork

In shadows where legends dwell,
Wrought iron gleams, casting a spell.
Ancient tales in metal are told,
Each curve a secret, each edge bold.

Beasts of yore in designs confined,
In every link, a story entwined.
Giant and sprite, side by side,
Emblems of dreams where wonders bide.

The hammer's song, the anvil's beat,
Crafting magic in rhythmic heat.
A smith's hands dance with fire bright,
Forging the dusk and the starlit night.

Whispers of steel in twilight's breath,
Binding the living, bridging the death.
In every artifact, a soul contained,
Myth and metal, forever chained.

A tapestry of time unfurls,
As iron bends and the legend swirls.
Emblems rise from the depths of lore,
In the heart of the forge, forevermore.

Cages of Whimsy and Restraint

Within whimsies, bright and fair,
Dreams are caught in gilded snare.
Jacobs of laughter, bars of despair,
A dance of shadows in the air.

A carousel of joys, we ride,
Yet hearts retreat, nowhere to hide.
Each twist of fate, a bittersweet song,
In the cage where the lost belong.

Ribbons of sorrow, threads of glee,
Weaving the fabric of what must be.
In a world of whimsy, lost in chains,
Each smile hides the weight of pains.

A flicker of hope, a tenuous spark,
In this cage of light, we dare embark.
With each tick of time, we learn the art,
Of holding the shadows close to the heart.

Yet through the bars, the laughter twirls,
Cages collapse and the magic unfurls.
In the embrace of whimsical restraint,
A paradox penned by fate's own paint.

The Dance of Nature's Grasping Talons

In the forest deep, where secrets lie,
Nature whispers with a feathered sigh.
Branches stretch like fingers wide,
Grasping at dreams as shadows glide.

The dance begins, a wild embrace,
Where earth and sky meet in a race.
Wings unfurl, talons gleam bright,
In a whirl of motion, pure delight.

Beneath the moon, in spectral light,
Creatures of night take elegant flight.
Every rustle, a lover's refrain,
In the heart of the wild, nothing is vain.

With each heartbeat, the rhythm flows,
In the grasp of the talons, nature grows.
A symphony sung in whispers and growls,
As the forest rejoices, echoing howls.

Yet in this dance lies a delicate thread,
Of life entwined with the dreams we tread.
In nature's arms, no fear shall remain,
Held safe in the dance, losing the pain.

Currents of Destiny in Metal's Embrace

In the forge of time, the metals meld,
Destinies whispered, secrets held.
Steel and fire, a fateful kiss,
In the crucible of dreams, find your bliss.

Flowing rivers of molten flame,
Etching our fates, carving a name.
With each spark, a choice is made,
In destiny's grasp, we are remade.

An echo of thunder, a clang of might,
In the heart of the forge, darkness turns bright.
With every hammer, the soul ignites,
Born from the shadows, into the light.

The current pulls, a magnetic force,
Guiding our paths without remorse.
Bound in iron, yet ever so free,
The dance of destiny, pure jubilee.

Hold tight to dreams, forged in your heart,
From the currents of fate, we never part.
In metal's embrace, let your spirit roam,
For in every creation, we find our home.

Echoes of the Earthbound Symphony

In the valley, the whispers roam,
Soft as the beating heart of stone.
Trees sway gently, in harmony's thrall,
Nature's voice sings, a resonant call.

Clouds gather close, like stories untold,
Casting shadows in shades of gold.
The brook chuckles, secrets it keeps,
While the moonlight into the silence creeps.

Across the fields, the breezes weave,
Through the tall grasses, they gently cleave.
With every note, the tremors of old,
Stir the earth as symphonies unfold.

In twilight's embrace, the stars ignite,
Mapping dreams in the velvet night.
And echoing softly, the Earth can sing,
In perfect balance, a wondrous thing.

The Sway of the Eldritch Embrace

In shadows deep, where whispers dwell,
The air is thick with an ancient spell.
Twisted trees reach with crooked hands,
Guarding secrets of foreign lands.

Faded voices murmur in gloom,
Echoing through the forgotten room.
A dance of phantoms, a spectral waltz,
Where time itself finds its own faults.

Mist curls tight, like a lover's sigh,
Enfolding dreams that wander high.
The moon peeks down with curious eyes,
Unveiling truths in silvery lies.

Winds howl softly, a mournful tone,
Binding souls who tread alone.
In the heart of night, an embrace so tight,
Holding shadows that drift from light.

Clay and Claw Entwined in Passage

In the quiet marsh, where secrets breathe,
Ancient tales through the waters seethe.
Footsteps whisper on the muddy banks,
Nature clothed in its earthy swanks.

Dragons of mud, with eyes so bright,
Stirring the currents under moonlight.
Fingers of clay, reaching for the sky,
As the night sings a lullaby.

With each gentle tug, the earth replies,
In the water's depths, their spirit flies.
Intertwined destinies, claw and earth,
In this passage of life, they find rebirth.

Beneath the surface, where the shadows tread,
Tales of ancients silently spread.
And in the stillness, so profound,
Harmony spins, where lost is found.

Wings of Fury in the Twilight Shade

In the twilight, where shadows wane,
Creatures stir with a sense of disdain.
Wings that flutter in a stormy dance,
Chasing echoes of a lost romance.

Furious winds howl through the trees,
Carrying tales on the trembling breeze.
A tempest unleashed, wild and free,
With razor-edged wings that long to flee.

Beneath the thick cloak of the darkening sky,
A symphony swells as the shadows fly.
With each beat of wings, a tale unfolds,
Of fierce-hearted souls, brave and bold.

In the throes of night, the world ignites,
Fueled by the fury of potent rites.
And as the echoes of winged hearts fade,
A new dawn rises, from twilight's shade.

The Lament of Unbroken Chains

In shadows deep, the echoes cry,
When dreams are bound, and hopes must die.
A heart entwined in sorrow's wake,
Yet still it yearns, for freedom's sake.

The chains that rattle in the night,
Speak of a past that feels so tight.
With every breath, a silent plea,
To break the bonds and just be free.

The whispers haunt, like ghosts they moan,
In every corner, fear has grown.
But deep inside, a spark remains,
A flicker bright amidst the chains.

For once the soul has tasted flight,
It dances with the stars at night.
Though shadows loom and clouds may swirl,
The heart will fight, unleash its pearl.

So let the chains be forged anew,
With bonds of hope and vision true.
Though heavy hangs the weary frame,
The spirit sings, and love's the flame.

The Fables of Feathered Restraint

In quiet glades where whispers dwell,
The tales of wings begin to swell.
With colors bright, the birds take flight,
Yet some must stay to face the night.

The fables weave of lost delight,
Of dreams that fade in waning light.
With feathers clipped, they long to soar,
To find the skies they knew before.

Yet wisdom speaks through muted tones,
In sorrow's grasp, they find their homes.
For in the bonds of earth and stone,
The strength of heart is truly grown.

Through trials faced beneath the morn,
The souls arise, anew reborn.
And though they crave the open air,
The ground holds roots, with tender care.

So let the fables take their flight,
In every heart, a spark of light.
For freedom sung, may yet be found,
In chains of love, our spirits bound.

Crumpled Leaves Beneath the Weight

In autumn's grasp, the leaves do fall,
Like whispers soft, they heed the call.
Crumpled dreams beneath the trees,
With every gust, they bend and freeze.

Each fragile skirt of rust and gold,
Holds stories of the brave and bold.
But burdens weigh, and hopes may fade,
As seasons change, and paths are laid.

Yet in their crumpled, withered state,
There lies a beauty, not of fate.
For every crack and every crease,
Holds echoes of a sweet release.

So gather 'round, and do not mourn,
For in the leaf, new life is born.
With winds that shift and skies that weep,
The stories of the past, we keep.

With every leaf that falls from grace,
A memory hugs the hollow space.
And though they crumble, look anew,
For underneath, the green breaks through.

Heartstrings in the Clutches of Fate

In twilight's glow, the heartstrings tug,
As fate weaves threads, both tight and snug.
Each pulse a note in life's grand song,
Through laughter's cheer and sorrows long.

When shadows creep and silence reigns,
The heart knows well its whispered pains.
Yet in the dark, a beacon glows,
A warmth that only hope bestows.

For every twist the journey takes,
The heart withstands, though surely aches.
In clutches strong, the will holds fast,
Through tempests wild, the die is cast.

With threads of trust that intertwine,
In fate's embrace, the stars align.
A tapestry of joy and strife,
Weaving the patterns of our life.

So let the heartstrings softly sing,
In courage found within the ring.
For though fate's hand is swift and bold,
The heart's own tale is yet retold.

Metalworks of the Wild's Embrace

In the forest deep where shadows play,
Old dragons breathe their fire in sway.
Forge of secrets, songs entwined,
With whispers of the ancients, intertwined.

Crafted by hands unseen, yet bold,
Metal glimmers with stories untold.
Beneath the boughs where magic weaves,
Their clamor dances, the heart believes.

Iron and oak in tangled dreams,
Rustling leaves sing of moonlit beams.
The creatures gather, their eyes aglow,
In this wild embrace, new tales will grow.

Blades of silver, shields of light,
Beneath the stars, the woods ignite.
Echoes of laughter in starlit nights,
Crafted by time, the heart ignites.

Now hear the call of the quiet stream,
Where shadows dance and fireflies gleam.
In unity's bond, the wild does bind,
Forging a legacy forever entwined.

Chronicles of the Fox's Grip

In twilight's hush, the world takes flight,
Cunning whispers, hidden from sight.
A fox creeps softly, with eyes like fire,
Chasing secrets that never tire.

Tales of mischief and trickster's art,
Woven in shadows, they twine the heart.
On moonlit paths, adventure stirs,
Life unfolds in the softest purrs.

Through bramble and thicket, the journey flows,
With each playful leap, the mystery grows.
In the dance of dusk, every leap and bound,
Holds echoes of laughter that linger around.

Fleeting moments, captured in time,
A melody sung in the fox's rhyme.
With every glance, secrets unfold,
In the chronicles, both wild and bold.

So follow the path where the wild things roam,
In the fox's grip, you've found your home.
Each whisk of the tail, each glittering eye,
Draws you into the night's sly lullaby.

Beneath the Watchful Terrestrial Eye

The mountains stand with wisdom vast,
Glancing down on the tales amassed.
Beneath the gaze of the earth's embrace,
Nature breathes in a sacred space.

Rippling waters reflect the sky,
Where dreams awaken and hearts can fly.
A silent guardian watches near,
Holding secrets far and sheer.

Underneath the stars, the world unfolds,
In the tapestry of life, all is told.
Every rustle bears witness to time,
In nature's arms, every soul can climb.

With roots that stretch in timeless grace,
Trees stand tall, a steadfast pace.
In their shadows, the stories dwell,
Of laughter and sorrow, of magic's spell.

So linger below this watchful eye,
Let the whispers of nature lift you high.
Embrace the wonder, the stories wide,
In the heart of the earth, let your spirit glide.

Stitching Dreams in Twilight's Loom

In twilight's glow, where dreams align,
The loom spins softly, fate's design.
Threads of starlight and whispers true,
Weave together the old and new.

With gentle hands, we stitch the night,
Creating patterns, woven in light.
In the tapestry of hopes and fears,
Each color tells the story of years.

As shadows dance and whispers play,
The loom of twilight holds sway.
Golden threads of wishes shared,
In each entwined fiber, love is declared.

In the silence, the heart beats strong,
Every weave a note in life's song.
With each soft pull, our dreams take flight,
In twilight's embrace, we turn to light.

So gather 'round as the night unfolds,
In the magic of stories that never grow old.
Stitch your dreams in the luminous loom,
Where hope is reborn, and sorrows consume.

www.ingramcontent.com/pod-product-compliance
Ingram Content Group UK Ltd.
Pitfield, Milton Keynes, MK11 3LW, UK
UKHW021508290125
4356UKWH00031B/308